At Home In Bell Buckle

Poems by Leona Elen

The Brideswell Press

For my mother, Florence, my daughter, Kim-Ellen,
and my husband Richard — a Mighty Trio of Support
…and in memory of Tom Buchan — poet, Scot and dear friend.

First published 1996 in the United States of America
by The Brideswell Press, Bell Buckle, TN 37020.

Library of Congress Catalog Card Number: 95-96042

ISBN 0-9649553-0-X

Printed in the United States of America
by Lewisburg Printing Company, Lewisburg, TN 37091

Designed and typeset in Adobe Garamond
by Richard Elen at The Brideswell Press.

CONTENTS

About the Author

LEONA ELEN (*née* Graham) BA Hons., MA, grew up in Nova Scotia and Ontario, Canada; took her degrees in English at the University of Western Ontario; lectured at the University of Victoria, British Columbia; and continued with PhD studies at the University of British Columbia, Vancouver. Exchanging her budding academic career for a lifetime of educational pursuits, her agendas became self-made and spiritually-motivated. Poetry, most ancient of literary arts, was her first love; thus it is only fitting that poetry comprises her first published book.

In the Sixties, like many other activists of her generation, she sought spiritual meaning in the company of like-minded souls. By the Seventies, this had led her to that most famous of all spiritual communities, the Findhorn Foundation in north-east Scotland, where co-operation with Nature is a guiding force. Working closely with two of the co-founders, she lectured, gave workshops and organized international conferences. By the late Eighties, she had found her way to that other great British community, Glastonbury – the ancient Avalon – a place of pilgrimage long before it became the first Christian settlement in England. With colleagues, she helped found the educational Isle of Avalon Foundation and the Library of Avalon. She also participated in the environmental movement, running for the Green Party in the Parliamentary election of 1992.

Leona's recent move to Tennessee with her husband Richard, has inspired her, finally, to publish. Several works are in the making, including a modern epic on an ancient theme, *Passages About Gwenhwyfar – A True Tale of Arthur's Queen.*

About The Brideswell Press

THE AIM OF THE BRIDESWELL PRESS is to produce and publish a series of inspiring works – works imbued with spiritual wisdom, to uplift and bring joy to the hearts and minds of all those who come into contact with them.

The name Brideswell indicates the dedication of the Press to the immanent presence of Brigit, Celtic fire goddess, inspiratrix of Christian and non-Christian alike; 'Bride' is one of Brigit's many names, indicating her link with the feminine/masculine mysteries, whereby the 'bride' (the goddess who may also manifest as the magical mare) is served by the groom, with all the inherent sexuality of such an alchemical union. Brigit is, in addition, a goddess of wells, guardian of those access points on the land where we draw up 'the waters of life'. In these days when the old wells have been covered, desecrated, destroyed and polluted, an awareness of these mysteries is crucial. By dedicating our Press to Her Being, we honor spirituality, sexuality and the sacredness of the Land and Waters that nourish and keep us.

The Subject Matter is unlimited, with an underlying foundation of 'The Sacred'. Genres include poetry, fiction, non-fiction; screenplays for feature films and television; compact discs; and other media.

INTRODUCTION

This small work measures a great distance covered.

I like to think my life is about service. Perhaps it began when I first experienced mystical visitations and flights into other worlds when I was very young, or further back, in my mother's womb, awaiting entry, when the entire world was at war, with so much death and destruction. Why incarnate at such a time if not to serve humanity, all life, the planet? They surely needed servers, apparent from endless conflicts finally escalated into lethal twentieth century warfare. Had we 'war babies' (as we grew up knowing ourselves, being called) foreseen the explosion of the atom and later, the hydrogen bomb, as later children foresee space wars?

How to serve?

Raised a lackadasical Protestant, I tried to turn into a Catholic nun. Denied, I understood God wanted me to enter into life whole-heartedly. I joined the Navy but bolstered myself with two and two thirds academic degrees, got pregnant at 23, married a sailor, bore my only child into the love-drunk sixties, and cunningly landed a university lectureship—just to keep the balance. Transforming into a political activist and feminist and teaching throughout the following years fulfilled my need to serve. I put academia aside and went for more radical alternatives, joining the educational-cum-spiritual Findhorn Community in Northeast Scotland in 1975, dedicating myself to cooperating with nature, treating all fellow humans as family, living love in action in a small community.I travelled a lot, freed myself from customary boundaries, making global contacts. It's been more than worth it, however insecure the lifestyle.

At Findhorn I discovered the Network of Light, people, places, communities, around the globe where a 'higher consciousness' was forming, encompassing Christian and non-Christian alike. A gathering of servers. Led to Glastonbury, England, the British cradle of Christianity and before that, Celtic religion, I met my present partner. Together we served in the community for a magical seven years.

When I landed in Bell Buckle, Tennesee, recently, I sensed the Soul of Turtle Island (North America) had called me home. Almost twenty years abroad had dissipated my Canadian identity; what remained was distrustful of being converted into an 'American', somehow associated with a seductive accumulation of wealth or a terrifying decline into poverty, a land of dreams and nightmare. My patriotic father's traditional dislike of Yankees had been a potent force in my youth. Memories cling. We had taken a shortcut to the Maritimes; when we crossed the border we kids were obediently sick to our stomachs. Not to speak of Dad's near fatal interchange with an American border guard when he confiscated us kids' Florida (!) oranges.

A few years previously, my guidance (intuitions received from my Higher Self in contact with Universal Mind) suggested my partner needed to make a serious career shift *with my support*. Else, possibly, would we be tempted to to take our involvement in Britain's environmental politics too seriously? Service has many faces.

When I got to Bell Buckle, scouted by my worthy pardner, I found a whole welcoming community of wild independents, eccentrics and good plain folks. This was not the America I had been raised to uselessly resent. Anyway, as it turned out, many of my best friends in Canada were Yankees converted to nominal Canucks.

But this was The South. Another Country. What would Dad have thought? Every day I see men in pickups who are the spitting image of him—so potent is the Scots-English gene pool. Britain supported the South in the Civil War. In the Revolutionary War Native Americans and unlucky 'United Empire Loyalists' supported the British; many of the latter fled to Canada, especially Ontario, where they make up a substantial backbone of Canadian society (thus the traditional distrust).

I had come home to Turtle Island with my heart open. The vow of service to Spirit ensures great adventures.

People have always been my priority. I am an eager catalyst for change. Producing my own work has always come last—after serving friends, cooking, cleaning up, paying bills... Literature has been a part of my life ever since I was wee bluenoser (Nova Scotian). It was always just beyond me, to really make it happen. Afraid of success *and* failure ? A demonic voice would intercede, "Another book? There are so many. It's all been said before."

But not by me to you, is my answer now.

Living here in Bell Buckle has proven to be a second birth—midwife to my second half-century of service. This little volume of grassroots poetry comes from my immediate response to you, the people and environment of Bell Buckle, Tennessee, the South and that mysterious and ever-shifting chalice that barely contains them, the USA.

I hope it serves you all as well as you all serve me.

"We're All Family…"

Just a few of our friends & family in Bell Buckle
– at least, a few of our friends & family of whom we had photographs…!
(Thanks to you all, whether we have a picture of you or not.)

PART I: FAMILY

House of Spirits

for Jocelyn

When I came here you were waiting to greet me at the door
You had arranged for us to be here
Perhaps I saw your shadow on the floor

When we leave here the task beset us will have been done
We will close the door behind us
We will return the key to your first son

Here is your House of Spirits and you the keeper still
I hear the music by the doorway
Dark birds light on the window sill

Some days I hear you clearly as if you've come to tea
The doorstep feels your footstep
But it is only the cat and me

Sweet spirit, since you wander may I put you at your ease
The door is bright with angels
Beyond is Heaven's House of Spirits, and they have come to please

Land Lady

for Rosanna

Walks in beauty
Unbelieving
Casts her spell
Unbinding
Blows her cover
Unerringly

A lady of the land

Land Lord
for Spencer

A first son, trapped
In bitter times, when land
Is measured by big bucks

Gentle man, tortured
By false values, when worth
Is counted by the clock

Carpenter of note,
He has a way with wood,
Builds firm foundations

Embracing the land
His wife holds so dear
His children grow upon

An uncommon man,
Of open mind and cast
At one with earth and sky

May your voice be heard
Inspired by God above
Lord of the land you love

The Maiden
for Hilary

A shy girl, a magical maiden,
Mirroring the mothers before her,
The matrix goddesses are made of,
The potent matter of men's dreaming

Artemis to my Aphrodite
Bearing witness to beauty of beasts,
Rhiannon, First Lady of the Celts,
Riding her white horse into the sea

Stepping into Medusa's lair
Of womanhood, quite bewildered
At the dark disorder of it all,
Wond'ring at the wilfulness of fate.

What goddess can your mother call hers,
All rednut brown to your gentle hue,
Flashing brave-hearted down life's broad highroad
Daring the Old, taking on The New

Demeter to your Kore.
Take care Persephone;
The underworld is deep
Demanding mortality

Penelope awaits Ulysses
Ereshkigal her sister Inanna
And deathly Kali young Pandora
The pomegranate your sweet tongue

Ride well the fair fields
Where black-eyed Susans
Run tall above you
Gather the sunflowers

Let the cunning fox be your eagle eye
The mildmost hare your persuasive ear
Hold the silver horn of the unicorn
In your honeysweet hands, and fly free

The Warrior
for Zeb

When they asked "Where will you go?"
He answered "Back home to Ta-na-si."

Though heaven offered many options
To a lad so filled with spirit as was he

Once upon a time
Before time was trapped, when the medicine wheel turned round
The woodland warrior killed for his family and his clan
Life was hard but full and he died nineteen summers young

Many times he passed this way and was always wise with wood
Many times he lit his hearthfire on this good and sacred ground
Many times he fought and died and came again to Ta-na-si

He was brown; he was black; he was white; and always red
Blood on the dying field, a gunshot through his head
Always he left his body here upon the land close to his heart

So when I see his trophies, be they arrows, guns or bows
I do not see the killer but the boy behind the flag
Fighting for his kinfolk, dying for The Land

But now a time is coming when the warrior will wake
And put aside his armaments and step a different pace
For it is The Land itself he lives for, not the glory of the chase.

A Brit Abroad

for my husband Richard

He's a wonder of a man, most truly,
Some women friends would clone him if they could
Though he's set in parts and his hair's unruly
And he wants to spend more than he should

But he's a Brit abroad and so he would

He's tall, dark and have some, as he says,
And he makes the woman in his life Mistress
Of all he owns and earns, so what a jewel!
Far superior to a necklace of finest pearl

For he's a Brit abroad and gives a girl a whirl

He's spiritually inclined and that's worth more
Than any other single attribute or score
For together we travel a path of love and light
With sunfilled wonders unfolding left and right

And he's a Brit abroad in whom I do delight

Photo of Richard by Leona

Deer Woman
for Elizabeth

The forest is black but the stars are shining.
Deer Woman walks carefully through the underbrush.
Beautiful, gentle, delicate, fine-boned.
Eyes wide with the wonder of life, whatever the danger.

She carries a clear impression of her destination.
Not to be dissuaded from the thorny path
She has left the herd to wander where she wills
Ever listening to her instinct that man kills

The moonlight catches her and in the darkness
She is transformed into the mythic beast
Her sable coat a silvery whiteness glow
Her little horns a healing spiral grow

This is who she is but can the hunter see?
Or are his eyes too filled with flesh?
Around Deer Woman spins a soft pale gold cocoon
Set there before the origins of man.

The hunter has no maiden to enhance his life.
Yet another skin or horn or thigh is naught
Without the sense of purpose that real life brings.
Deer Woman dances in his sight, he lowers his guard

And from his head the staghorns sprout
And bushy beard turns all to fur
On all four legs he runs to her
And begs her have him for her husband man

Man you are and man you aren't
Says sweet unicorn to stunning stag
He cannot see what he's become
He left his dog, he left his gun

For you I will be deer again said she
All gold and silver in the shining night
Together we shall breed anew
And in our mating leave our world a clue.

Queen Anne's Lace
for Anne

Lady of Lace, Queen of Hearts
Commanding the countryside
Prolific and austere, forever young

She models the world within her,
Draws in the passers-by,
Demands the best, the rest may pass on by.

Her court is full of joy and colour.
She stands apart, mixes in, disappears.
Her word is law and love in action.

Her needs few, desires plenty
Artfulness acute
Her being fulsome, becoming her

We fluttering ladies-in-waiting
Grow bright in the light about her
We come and go, she stays to grace the greensward

Southern Belles and Spirit Cavaliers
for my newfound sisters & brothers

We have come amongst you,
Avalonian mists streaming behind us,
Planetary futures deepening before us.

Bright stars in indigo skies
Faded confederate flags
Fluttering in the warm breeze.

Your spirit cavaliers did not abandon you,
Though Eagle Masters did wreak their revenge,
Your blood lines mixed inextricably

May you bring to these outlaw nations
A renovated sense of righteousness
Cleansed of mere religion, base politics and greed.

In the dawning and dusking of honour
The cardinal wisdom of the heart shall prevail
Your beauty and grace the measure of all things

Learned Ladies
for Judy

We are learned ladies
And not from Xanadu
Mistresses of many arts
Though some are through
Washing dirty dishes
And baking pecan pies

We are learned ladies
Who cannot count the cost
Of lifetimes spent or lost
Ferreting out wisdom
From Halls of Higher Learning
Keeping Sophia's fire burning

We are learned ladies
Education is our game
Patience is our name
Bureaucracy has bored us
Since Sappho penned her poems
Since Mother Earth made biomes

Whither did we wander
When we left our cloister walls?
Whether we played mistress,
Maid or nanny, schoolmarm
Or ruling governess
We were deep within us
Learned ladies everyone

Now the times go turning
We worry what will come.
Women of tomorrow
Stand upon our shoulders
Take what you can borrow
Move aside the boulders

Join us learned ladies
And walk toward the sun
Our work is not yet done
Busy in our office
Or in our studio
Baking bread, breeding roses
Bless the learned ladies, everyone

Lady of the Grail
for Jeanette

You made a plate of clay and marked it with fruits
It seemed so simple and we were all at play
But your plate in life is full in deed
And you would have it graced with gold
Every day at work in your café you carry platters
Serving thousands—you work to live
But work is deeper than we conceive
This plate this platter this holy grail you serve
We women are the vessels and we pour out our love
We arrange it for the delectation of our beloveds
The children of our wombs unto the end of time

When from abroad came a stranger
Who nearly speaks another tongue
But you are patient and do offer her
The gift of love that comes with an open heart
For she is but a passer-by who's lost her spindle
And left her besom[1] in some distant land
By day she spins her wordloom to fox the wolf
Whilst at night she dreams midwifery,
Of passageways into the heartland
Where monsters and miracles are born and die
Where the real battles are fought and won

O lady of the grail you did mistake me
For another whose face I do not know
When you see me now I see you see me
You have understood why I have come
To sit amongst the ladies of the court
To tell stories and to mumble of my mission
You walk in grace all unknowing of your wisdom
Your smile lets me see into your golden heart
The red cross knight is surely near you
To protect you from all ill and dark despair
This is the least that he must do to serve you

The time will pass and we will leave you
Passing into other lands to other pilgrim tasks
But you will stay to pass the grail and heal the hurt
You will do as you have been guided to
There is a learning passing through you now
That comes from pain and labor at the cost of life
It will pass and you will mend you and carry on
You will fill the empty platter and serve the plate
You are all women who serve and carry on
You break my heart but you mend it too
O lady of the grail may life honour you

[1] A 'besom' is an old Somerset broom made of willow. I left mine in a friend's care but it was recently brought over to me by an Angel; women and brooms is a fascinating study; female witches' associations with brooms is based on the need of good housewives to cleanse their homes of unwanted dirt and critters

Running As One
for Jere, Master Runner

Do you remember, brother, how we knew this land by foot?
Before horses ran among us, before we wore the boot?
The trackways were well-travelled, our villages kept informed
Before forests became timber, before The Circle was malformed

The mounds rose high above us and we entered up with awe
For there the shaman awaited us to tell him what we saw
We ran perfect as one body for from one womb we came
They chose us before our birthtime for mother dreamt our Name

Running As One we wandered this country far and wide
We vowed to run together until the day we died
But I was born a woman and you were born a man
So in the end our lives were run by dictates of The Plan

For though Our Run was paramount, my body blossomed forth
And I was chosen then to mate with a shaman of the North
And in all the lives that I have lived in northern climes apart
I looked to see if I could find my former counterpart

Then I remembered who we were, that night, in the old Café
When you touched my wrist and said, you have a runner's way.
I have my loving brothers, they are all three runners, true
But now our vow is honoured, I have a newfound friend in you.

The Florence Factor
for the two Florences

They span two generations, one continent,
Two nations but one culture despite dissent,
One is my mother, but both are my friend
I owe them more than I could ever lend

Each one has been a mother first and foremost
But all along their life they marked the milepost
Mindful of their need to seek the innermost
Meaning, adventuring to the furthest outpost

The one reminds the other that her journey's just
The very start to a pilgrimage she must trust
Maybe it's better to burn out than rust
Fight for freedom of the mind than just adjust

One is still dark of hair and one is now white
Both retired from working where might was right
But not alright. Both await the coming night
Alive and vibrant and beautifully bright.

The Wisdom Circle

March 6, 1995
on the occasion of the latest and longest Space Shuttle voyage
and the latest gathering of our women's group

Round and round we spin
on this small and beautiful blue globe
wondering why and who we are
sending messengers into space
with very large glasses from which to drink the mysteries deeper*

we sit round and full ourselves
women of age, aging wonderfully
we whisk the eggs in our bowls
we women of many colours
Scots, Irish, English, Cherokee, Ojibwa, Mexicali
we call ourselves Americans, Canadians, Europeans

Intent on a new kind of revelation
we ponder more than mere phenomenon
connecting the red wool gathering us
we go where others firmly trod before us
etching our descendants' destinies
red clay bodies moulded to time's tuning
a river of ancestral drums pouring into Mary's sea

In the south and of it we hear the cicada sing
the cricket play the cardinal rule the blue bird shy
none of us are what we seem
hostessing our dreams, harnessing our days
we are a magnificent team
open and ready for the bigger business of spiritual dressage
we shall walk or gallop and pay the cost
we are we are not the coffee spoon, we are the cup

we cannot stay we cannot leave
wisdom's way is to believe
now is forever
we
must
be
more
than
dust

*The Hubble Space Telescope

The Wisdom Circle At Work

We meet on Mondays and we turn around
The clocks that say this time or that
The calendars that claim to know the date
Immortality is not an issue and we are innocent of guile.
But we are ancient women becoming Wise Crones
And we meet just as our mothers did and daughters will.
Some make quilts, some study the Bible, some bake,
Some feed the poor, some save the arts, some sing.
We meet together and we do every sort of thing

We make finger pots of clay dug from the ground of Tennessee
Remembering those who went before us who did just this, as we.
We mould lotus and sun,
Angel face and lady of the kiln, our holy grails.
We talk up storms and smooth the seas.
We learn to listen and interrupt with grace
We drink and eat and pass the mirror round
Tell tales, commiserate and make some clear decision.
But best of all, we sit together in a circle to share, envision

The Matriarch
for Frieda H.

She raised her children well
Enough to ensure they pursued their dreams
As best they could
It being America and all the rest, the best

She loved her garden
And still flowers grow alongside her pathway
But you can tell gardening is no longer
The meaningful occupation it once was

She has a large house, even now
So that the grandchildren can stay
And play, so she has room to breathe
In, to be the fine lady she really is

She shows up to hear Marty sing
And have lunch with the ladies
Of Bell Buckle and abroad,
Keeping her eye on her small community

She suffers from numerous ailments
But she runs them, not the reverse,
And she enjoys the caretaking
Abilities of her son and daughter

She catches my eye and smiles
Whenever we meet, and I am aware
That there is more to her than meets
The eye, as her sister's daughter says

These may be her autumn years
But she will have her way with them
She is considering all that came before
And measuring up the count as to the cost

Now, she can speak and say as she wills
And wants, she's done her time
And paid her dues. I salute her
For behind her studied deameanour

Lies much that was and could have been—
The matriarch embodied
In our time, bearing good news
But reminding us of the simple nature of sacrifice

Did Mary Really Get the Best Part?
for Martha

She stood for Christ
As she served them food and drink
She worshipped every word
Did Mary really get the best part?

Her role was clear
There was a living to be made
Duties to perform
Did Mary really get the best part?

Service is sacrifice
The yielding of the flesh to function
Involvement in the world
Did Mary really get the best part?

Sisters have a way of segregating
Taking turns to teach and learn
Resentment turns to recognition
Martha and Mary bless them both

Made All of Flowers She Was
for Chele

Not Brigit, nor Boadicca.
No Beatrice, but being all yourself.

And yet, some goddess guides you,
As you dance and sprite the day before you.

Perhaps in deed or mayhap
'Tis Bloeduewedd who tells your tale most truly.

A Brythonic web of Wales.
Herstory mine and yours. Made all of flowers she was

Bred for a god and hero.
Not for herself alone. She chose a man to live a life her own.

Magicians mad pursued her.
Through hill and dale, she fled. She rose.

Fore'er now the cunning owl,
Queen of the night, wings alight, wisdom's delight.

You wax and wane, disappear,
Returning with knowledge of other worlds

Reminding us the sun shines through the moon
In you the dark and light make fire bright

Jack of Wands
for George

Jack travels inner worlds, storyteller to those he can entice
He has the gift of sight, but he has no doubt paid a price
He has a sadness about him that sings of sacrifice.

He doesn't need a metal detector to unearth anything
Truer than a lie detector when it's time for truth to bring
He's an unsung shaman, without a rattle or feather wing

But he told me yesterday he has a wand, it's black and white.
Does it determine good from evil, light the way in the dark of night?
Did he offer me this magic wand, or did I get it right?

When you are speaking with him, you feel he's adding up your score,
Holding a mirror to your conscience you'd better not ignore.
When he's finished you feel a wee bit lighter than before

Marty says he takes up whatever you've been thinking through
Frieda brings him cups of custard which he offers back to you
One day he and Marty sang me a Beatles' song and it came true.

Calico Cat
for Pandora

A doubted gift, saved from the dogs.
Delivered from a running engine, descent unknown.

Dedicated to her litter and food trays
Determined to stay and be purrfect

A prosaic pussycat perhaps.

On another paw.

A precious little bundle of white and gold.
Presented with best intentions, her purpose clear.

Loves to play, snuggle and leap,.
Very verbal, vocabulary deepening by the day.

A poetic necessity perchance.

Impossible view of Bell Buckle's front row of stores.

Part II:
Friendly Fires

To the Angel of Bell Buckle
A Prose Prayer Poem

The days stretch before me, glorious and bright. When the rains come, they are welcome, the land drinks. I am content. Despite years of Britain's sodden pastures and dark clouds, a land still held in thrall to foreign gods.

Am I under some grand holy spell? Perchance an Angel has called me to this southern landscape, where turkey vultures make significant circles in the sky and flashing cardinals warn me of false steps.

Eagle Angel, you have called me to this place, so familiar now after mere months of attendance. The peach gold evening skies, the ebony dark, the balm of spring becoming. This atmosphere reeks of the nectar of the Sacred.

Re-self discovery is in the order of things.

My feet bare upon hot soil. Summertime memories of my childhood in continental Ontario.

All the creatures greet me, reminding me of other, more ancient times, before the stench of car and the distant drone of plane.

Your guidance is welcome in this time of grace. The same guidance, the same grace surrounding me upon arrival in the Findhorn Community in Northeast Scotland and in The Ancient Avalon, Glastonbury, Somerset, England. First refinding, reawkening, the self experienced there long ago. The old stories, the old pains, enhanced by the passage of time, and then transcended.

With such reconnection arises a sweetness resembling the aroma from some forgotten flower first recognized in youth.

This time passes, too quickly.

The warrior returns, fighting battles to keep the land intact, honour rivers and trees, offer a just inheritance to children so they may raise children. So peace and prosperity will last beyond one selfish generation. All at the mercy of men lacking integrity, who have sold their souls to some disguised devil with a wily rationale. Their sleeping wives who support their husbands' false claim that land is theirs to do with whatever they will, with no counting the cost. Who have not made the link between the pocket book, the purse and the planet's resources. Whose green eyes belie their politics.

In the face of this certain righteous anger in the Temple of the Living Earth, I pray that this wondrous state of grace prevail to provide me with the strength to embody the courage and wisdom with which to understand and enact the task set for me at this time, in this sacred place.

At Home in Bell Buckle
for our friends here

Richard and I are happy in Bell Buckle.
We were an excellent choice for this special scene.
Thank you for welcoming us home.

We came from another magical place
Where golden apples fall eternal in green fields
Where poets mix with potters and the sun shines despite the rain

From thence unabandoned allies send messages of distress
Striving to calculate the measure of our move
Away from the Honey'd Isle* and The Ancient Avalon.

Somewhere, hidden in the soil of this hobbity scape
Or mayhap on some gnarled tree or stringy bush
There is a Bell that calls us Buckles back

Eight times a day the train from Out Of Time
Roars through the uncollapsing centre
Taking the tinkle of the Bell forth to an unsuspecting world

The notes are sweet, the tune an old one turned again
It is a rustic worn and aromatic town filled with itself
There's room for stress and turmoil and any matter of decline

*An ancient Celtic reference to Old Britain

But there is a strain within the buckling of her muse
That sings of other possibilities than heretofore remembered
What they portend the poet dares to see, the potter plots.

A city of the stars, a village of the worthy
Behind that quaint exterior, that holy town of yore
A cast of angels rehearses for the music of the spheres

Tongue in gear, they advance upon the tourist trade
Planting where others feared to plan
A most amazing garden of delights.

Back Streets of Bell Buckle
for Jere and Florence

The back streets of Bell Buckle
Are taut with change
As yet another new guard takes over from an old
Tall trees and trimmed lawns tell long tales
Haunted houses get facelifts and hysterectomies,
Like slaves long gone, they pass from one owner to another
Rise in value, shifting the ground beneath everyone
Dogs run mad from road to lawn to corner roundabout
Disappear and die or wisen up
Cats watch carefully from wicked verandahs and curtained windows
Birds whistle down seasons whilst ticks and other exotic insects
Proliferate despite home improvements and unnatural solutions
Here and there, one or two abandoned buildings
Point to poignant stories yearning to unfold
Entropy enfolds their wounded hearts
Lawns transformed into weed patches and thistledown fields
Victorian edifices intermix uneasily with rusting trailers
Elasticed in a timeless show of perfect resistance to poshness
Some properties signal suburban replants
There is a hush where once children must have played

The ghost of Sawney Webb runs through it all
His legacy a thriving runaway educational enterprise
Backing up real estate, bringing money to magic life
Reminding all of the right of the relatively rich to learn privately
Planked up against the right to be educated at all by all
After all, The American Dream Is the Right to Choose
Two, three, several communities interlock fitfully unwillingly
As the 21st century comes knocking at their doors
No supermarket, no fast food chains, no gas stations
In the front strip
Antiques, crafts, cafés, barber shop
Pull the pilgrim tourists into brief nostalgic dreams of yesteryear
Before driving home in air conditioned lead free covered wagons
With gratifying thoughts of pioneers and hard times passing by
Just long enough to justify the journey

If they took the time to walk the back streets
They would wonder at the measure of this town

being american
for Uncle Sam and e e

has something to do with an experiment in multiple paradigms
lots to do with seeing through them when their time is up

every american starts off with a sense that everything is possible
most americans end up misunderstanding limits to their growth

being american means a lot to those who buy, and fly their flag
but it hurts to have that underlying creed of greed unfurled

some americans will now no longer bask in baseball games
a few may now consider football in a judgmental light

being american is a show canucks and mexicans have tickets for
though they watch it quite differently from side galleries

all americans have some rights the world can be envious of
except their women's, whose era has not yet fully come to light

being american is a mixture of death-dealing pioneer mentality
and an urge to build, invent, to make the best the fastest biggest...

americans are a generous breed of every worldly culture
aliens pray you grant Gaia the full measure of wisdom won thereby

Beltane in Bell Buckle

(1) *Digression*

The weather augured ill.

Dark and forbidding southern skies loomed,
Daring us to produce a Beltane Fire.
After all, we were still strangers here,
Even our landlord, Tennessee born and bred,
Mix of Irish and Italian bloodstreams
—ours is a faded European facade on a backdrop of stolen land
—as Britain was taken from the Brython, Scotland from the Picts
and Scotti, Eire from the Irish, England from the Anglo-Saxons
—the story of land is the story of thievery, the dominion of war

But I digress into ancestral mummery

(2) *It's A Good Fire*

The weather augured ill.

Clouds encircled us as our local hero lit his message
                                        to the missing moon
The fire rose high, the biggest bonfire in Bell Buckle this year
But it's only Beltane Eve

And lots of time to plan bigger and better
To cast a fiery shadowagainst a coming of the doom
Behind the barn Davy Crockett pumps another round
                                        into his musket
Or is it only Zeb bouncing his basketball
The little maiden merry Matty fairy sprite dancing all about, her hair
haloed in the firelight

Digression comes at Beltane, as we fire up our souls
Diffusing our seed, planting our selves
Hoping for good crops come fall

We gathered, forsaking the easy clemency of the tall framed house
A neighbour came to question the bonfire, was it a bad one?
Buz knew the seeker, *No, he said, it's a good fire*
I said, it's a need fire, we're burning what needs to be burned
And anyway, a Bell Buckle fireman lit it, so it must needs be bonny
We have determined to be rid of all unnecessary waste
We have Gaian dispensation against more green house gas,
Just this night, the clouds will open, the stars shine through
The ancestors will watch us from the heavens, their souls freed
To wander in celestial delight, awaiting our delivery

They did. The clouds parted, the stars shone in a circle round
We gave thanks in wonder, though at first it seemed a little matter
Just consider what came before and after, thunder, torrential rain.
We did not part the clouds, they parted in our innocence
The Old Ones accepted our sacrifice, waste matter made sacred,
Two hot dogs slipped into the coals by seeming chance
Out of range of two ravenous real dogs
That heathen cat Pandora kept well away from our shenanigans
From Bel's good bonfire, misspelt Baal, jealous Jehovah's enemy,
                                        no less, no more

Religion passes for little at Beltane, the church doors creak
                    on rusty hinges, empty steeples rise high in Prideville
Though I noticed a Sunday or two ago that Mary
                                    is coming home to roost

We cooked vacuum-packed marshmallows on a newly patented
                                    device that you burn after use
We drank a bit of burgundy and we feasted from covered dishes
There wasn't another Beltane fire within known memory or space
But we re-set the abandoned clock of the seasonally sacred
be honest said Jere; Florence and I discussed liberal democracy
J Gregry was eminently quiet and thoughtful
Jeanette was a source of relish, sugar and spice
Elizabeth and Rosanna rediscovered the Land of Heroines
Richard would have sung Blake's Jerusalem if he'd been drunk
                                    or simply more inspired
By the old new need-fire Martha and her fiery-new-man resembled
dark Celtic gods disguised as good neighbours
Chele and Quentin were taking a pause from digging for treasure.
their eyes looking far distant in the fire's shadows

Somewhere the barn owls were watching us, but the bluebirds
                                    slept through it all
And where the cardinals have gone is a mystery
The imported starlings had shut up for the night
And the wise woodpecker had found a hole worth a while.
And this is only my first Beltane in Bell Buckle

Railroad Square – Helene Koppejan

Empire Days

These are the days of Empire

Too short for all the resources we've planned to squander
Too long if measured by the stress related to the task
Too full to understand what it is we must truly ponder

Parading others' injustice, keeping track little of our own
Discussing a lot openly, keeping secrets from ourselves alone
Overeating from choice or genes, whilst others starve to the bone

It is our turn at the planet's helm, making our world watch
It is a final examination that we dare not botch
We must learn what other imperialists never do:

Greed has limits, guns are lethal, God is on watch too

These are the days of Empire

When the truth would set us free if we could but find it
When freedom of the press makes wars a false slideshow
When Othello's tale rewound is Hollywood's latest hit

Fixated on our righteousness we mark our consumerist scorecard
Placated into platitudinous gestures we dance in contiguous lines
Convinced of Manifest Destiny we trample with mortal disregard

It is a time of plenty and poverty
It is a time of wealth and wrath to come
We must show what other conquerors failed,
                              our spiritual potentiality

Good is possible, grain is life, Earth is Empress,
                    Spirit the PayMaster of us all

Oklahoma

to the victims and survivors of the bombing

From nearby Tullahoma to distant Oklahoma
We grieve
For mindless men of violence have once again
Startled us into pain and dark confusion
We wonder what good can come of evil
When we are given the platitude to sup
We turn in our beds at night, imagining
The same for any one of us or ours
We are bereft of consolation or we are full
Our table is weighted down with suppositions
Right looks to left ashamed and left to right sanguine
Centrist nods her head in milky wisdom
Guns take on a glint as yet unseen or understood
And chemical fertilizer reveals its true payload
Army training is turned against us and talk hosts
Defend themselves against their bitter aims
We are born into a better world than many
We have more to eat and drink and be merry for
We are full to death and suffer from obesity
Whilst others starve and peer at us from tv screens
Whilst others die from weaponry we sold their enemies
Whilst others blame and envy us our way of life
That day five hundred lives were struck a blow
More than five thousand Rwandans suffered too
But ours are ours, those children, women, men
They are our next door neighbours here at home
Someday distant Rwanda may seem so too
But today is ours to grieve for ours
To hope the hate the 4000 pounds of bomb embodied
May dissipate, resolve into some other measure
More consequent of love and trust and truth
May all those men of violence who lie in little boys
Turn their anger and despair toward courage to do good

On a Southern Porch
for Bob S.

On a Southern porch
Comfortable with crafty cushions and a swing seat
Large soft armchairs and a bit of bubbly
Bubba alerts us to the rightward swing America is taking
Seeking to turn back the clock
And take its own manufactured cowboy nostalgia
Seriously, movies making still life seem alive
Amateurs try Xrated films on for real
Home is haunted with hanged men
Unhappy housewives and fearless teachers watch sons and students
Murdered in drive-by killings and classroom brawls
Daughters are raped twice-over, persuaded to bear unwanted children.
A little southern exposure comfort comes as slow-motion Baptists
Recall the nature of original sin, holding out on the rest
If they got what they think they want
They would hide in shame if they could remember
It was them who dun it
Rich or poor or in-between this mentality of fear and loathing
Falls like a cloak over the unsuspecting
Good Samaritans and bad alike
Sometimes I think I see the Evil One wandering the roads
Dropping his poison apple seeds into the manicured front yards
The beliefs of the faithful having finally brought him to life
He does well in the aisles of the ubiquitous supermarket
Where the many shop to the tune of a few
Wishing they could buy Everything
And move to the next level down
There is no point in raging
This war has been going on since time collapsed us into form
But with each birth we hope for the hundredth monkey
To wash her potato on the seashore
For the child to turn to his insatiate parent
And say "No more"
Eyes alight trailing rainbow skeins

Splitting open kinfolk
Spilling away the gross national product
Onto the dying streets of the planet
Whereupon trees blossom as once they did
And the poisoned earth and waters sparkle again
And the eyes of the Evil One will close for a thousand millenia
At least
And leave our descendants a heritage of heaven here and now

Carnton Plantation – a Southern porch poignant with sad memories of the Civil War. It is said that at one point five Confederate Generals lay dying there: the house had become a hospital.

Passing Through?
for Greg

Are we passing through this landscape
Is this our grand escape

Where dogs continue to chase cars
Where folks still go to church a lot
Where guys are lookin out for gals

Are we here to stay a bit and settle down
To understand the whyfor of this town

Why people honk as they pass by
Why our landlord is a genuine gent
Why his wife has a spiritual bent

Are we on a honeymoon cruise through time:
Recalling the value of a dime

That sense of righteousness that God is on our side
That belief in the illusion of free enterprise
That unawareness that everything has life and dies

Are we here like sliders from another world
Bringing the best from futures yet to unfold

The beauty of communities that hold their shape
The wisdom of the women who meet in peace
The strength of men who have gone beyond lend or lease

Are we stuck in a never ending spiel
Wild west rodeo, awaiting a better deal

Relief from taxes, politicians whom we can trust,
Cars that run forever, a system that is just…

Sawney Webb Passed This Way

for Quintin

Past the flow'ring redbud
Cows chewing on their cud
Down Adam's Road and hill
We drive to Shelby's Ville[1]

A blossoming white pear
Alongside Fairfield Pike
Graveyard plastic flowers
Eclips'd by daffodils

Was Billy Alexander
Polly Thickett's friend?[2]
Some old patriot's Parkway
Ensures we do not stray

Lawn blooms into meadow
Miss Daisy, Sir Dandelion overflow
Coop Road remembers Coop
Now few remember Coop[3]

Sawney Webb passed this way
Now it's Highway 82
Students of yesterday
Leave us golden memories too[4]

---

[1] Shelbyville is the nearest large settlement to Bell Buckle, named after Isaac Shelby, a Revolutionary soldier (and a former Governor of Kentucky) descended from a Welsh father, Evan Shelby, and once this settlement was called Shelby's Ville.
[2] Unlikely in fact since Billy was reputedly a hermit type character, but one never knows...
[3] There are still descendents of the Coops to be found in this area; the old Church at the crossroads memorialises many Coops
[4] Sawney Webb, founder of the prestigious Bell Buckle School, reputedly had his students plant the gorgeous array of daffodils along Highway 82 linking Bell Buckle to Highway 231; Highway 82, shown on the cover of this book, is called the Sawney Webb Memorial Highway

Sounds: Spider to Star

for Kim-Ellen

This is a new land still to us.
We listen to her sounds
Lest she abandon us to some lesser fate.

We are still white in her eyes.
Her sun is strong and hastens to deepen us
So we can walk the red road.

Lightning cracks us open
Thunder wakes us from temporary tombs
Tornadoes turn us inside out

Brilliant cardinal: wean us from our pale ghosts.

Coyotes come close to hunt us up.
Sacrificing themselves to warn of trickery.
Shrill sounds of jay and starling,
Lower octaves to hovering stillness of hawk and vulture.

Seductive cacophony of country music,
Translated tales from a nostalgic far eastern dream,
Holding, binding us to blood skeins.
Whilst red masters try the value of one hand held

The silent potent spider goddesses
live inside our computers, waiting to be heard
their sounds are long and trellis-like

Crawl and persevere

We heat our homes with long-dead trees and foliage
we deaden the air with lethal fume
plastics line our graves

there is no isolated place
no desolation, no empty space
no out in the middle of nowhere

Everywhere is home to someone, spider to star

Southern Belles
for my Wisdom Circle Sisters

Time has come round again in your favour
Scarlett has been reborn in her children
Her survivor's heart has blossomed forgiveness
In the bright eyes you bear witness through

Your mirrors may be edged in tarnished gold and bronze
Your combs broken, replaced by scrunchies
Your hearths transformed by microwaves and juice extractors
Your elegant slippers by bare-faced trainers

Yet your homes still welcome strangers of good heart
Your hospitality erasing differences of birth and circumstance
Your hearts crafted in the old arts displayed for all to see
Your handiwork tempered in the bodies of men and boys

Your daughters continue to remember the country
They speak in tongues little different from their grandmothers
They claim power and position with their northern sisters

they begin to embrace their darker sisters
who drive through their past in grandams and cadillacs
bright eyed children spilling from the windows of their mending hearts

Perchance I will stay to celebrate that day of reckoning
when all shall be forgiven all round
And new beginnings forged in sacred time and space
A bystander purchasing her ticket to this show
May pledged herself into a midwife's role
Assisting in the miracle of birth of a people and the land

More than black and white await redemption
in the fiery eyes of an eastern saint.
Far back beyond before Tanasi was,

here in the Cherokee homelands
Other daughters kept this hearthfire glowing,
watched its ashes scatter in the winds of change.

Your destiny is
More than a flag a battle a broken hoop

Will you birth from your holy womb incorporate
A world fit for the worthy and the brave?
Where warrior and poet walk side by side
Of the same body, the same mind, of the same spirit,
building the New?

The State of the Eagle
for Buz

What really endangers them is their ingenuous ingenuity
Which has brought them to this pass, this brink,
Why no one really measures up against them
When their soul shines out from ruffled breast and bright eye
Who can say where they will wander next,
Within or without, earth or space,
Whose cause will catch their far-seeing glance?
Whatever they do, driven by supply and demand
Whether just or not, Manifest Destiny is their willing code

Made from all sorts, mix of reptile and mammal,
Missing links, Matadors of the West moving ever onward
Magnified in the likeness of their god, omniscient,
Mellowing now, recovering from a Russian winter,
Magicians casting spells of free enterprise and money markets
Molecular comprehension making time travel relevant
Moribund paradigms abandoned to the gods of practicality
Maidens still sport on the green and lads lose their balls, but
Merry meet, merry part, the witches of Salem haunt them
Maybe Marilyn* was right, breathing conspiracy

Perhaps this is the greatest show on earth, now, anyhow
Parents and offspring promote the Piccadilly circus of talk shows
Predator hosts loosed from cages to immunize patients
Penthouses proliferate coming up trumps
Poor folks sleep in portals and prisoners get fried
Paramilitary meet with police force personnel
Poppycock says the President, perseverance furthers
Prickly pears and hot peppers are served for lunch
Pick-up sticks manage a comeback in the housing market
Pentecost came and went and Babel returns to the Bay,
Peering at the moon, watching his P's and Q's

Men are penetrating
Women particularly poignant
About being an endangered species

* References: (1) to Marilyn Ferguson's work *The Aquarian Conspiracy* where
she points out the semantic roots of the word 'conspiracy'. to breathe to-
gether; and (2) maybe the ghost of Marilyn Monroe about her death, being a
modern witch of sorts, able to seduce men of great power and prestige

Brigit's Well, Republic of Ireland

The One Work
for Lauren
The Climate Changes are come upon us
It is not that it has not rained so before
Tall tales from Texas and New Orleans tell truths
Few wish to announce
From the drifting housetops
From the sunken cellular carphones

Shall we wake to mend our dams before the greater storm
Own our negligence or preach another Noah's Ark
The signs are come. Recycling newspaper is not enough
Yesterday was VE Day
Everyday is Earth Day
My compost bin is paltry beside the problem at hand
The feast is over and the festival of repair must begin

I have begun to contemplate a Quantum Leap back into Time
To touch the minds of waste and rape
Perhaps it has already begun and my deep sleep foregone
We need no new enemies to focus our anger
Bombings will not assuage the pain of delivery of truth
The task is at hand and we must mobilize the troops
For the One Work
The children haunt us with their asthmatic eyes

The Party
for Bob T.

It was a party of all sorts, the second of its kind
We had indulged in, tasting Shelbyville's rich delights.
Roundabout the candybox we searched,
Finding old and new friends who might have been.

The garden all aglow with the labours of a faery princess,
White-gloved African queens smiling through their magic spell.

A basket-weaver poet told his tale, his French Lieutenant hers,
A tall Celtic goddess spoke in a wondrous way, all unknowing,
Whilst a woman from Tupelo Mississippi took my man in thrall.

Dark old men in suits, their wives waiting for death, controlled
The edges, the middle ground held by the mighty of that class,
But at the sticky core of that marshmallow spiral danced
The good god Pan himself, playing his windy pipes,
His satyrs and fauns etched against the moonlit night.

'Twas the place to be, that eve in Middle Tennessee,
Skirting porch and garden, delving into rooms full
Of folk proudly descended from backwoods cabin life ,
Country cottages left on faraway shores or dark satanic mills,
Strong faces, filled with shame and hope, ancestors in their eyes.

There was General Bragg[1], enraged in ravaged retreat,
His pretty prisoner Pauline[2], the actress playing spy,
The noble Forrest[3] born and raised in Bedford's backwoods
Deepset hawkeyes remindful of the misery of that uncivil war,
Davy Crockett[4], taking his tall tales as far as Washington,
Thomas Bedford Jr[5], revolutionary soldier from the War before,
Mary Dobson[6], widow woman thrice, lucky twice

Did they stand beside me, were their shadows on the wall,
Did I imagine their laughter at the wonder of it all
That such a party in such a town could take place at all
Without their being party to the history of it all?

[1] General Braxton Bragg, the Confederate General who was forced to retreat
from Murfreesboro, set up headquarters (with General Leonidas K. Polk) in
Shelbyville and was later forced from thence as well
[2] Major Pauline Cushman *(left, below)* who acted as a spy for the Unionists
and was imprisoned at Shelbyville and condemned to death by a court martial
but the 'liberation' of Shelbyville in June 1863 by General Granger's forces
came just in time to save her life
[3] General Nathan Bedford Forrest, the legendary Civil War Confederate
Calvaryman, born July 13, 1821 in a frontier cabin near Chapel Hill, then
part of Bedford County (of which Shelbyville is the county seat)
[4] David Crockett *(right, below)* made one of his homes on the headwaters of
Mulberry Creek, (1811-15) where it is said that he got his reputation for
being a notable backwoodsman
[5] Thomas Bedford Jr, after whom Bedford County was named (a Virginian);
enlisted in the Revolutionary War on February 5, 1776, promoted to lieuten-
ant and then captain, refusing further promotion to fulfil his promise to the
mothers of his company's men that he would see them personally through the
war; he emigrated to East Nashville and then south to Rutherford County
[6] Mary Dobson, a pioneer Shelbyville woman, married thrice, twice to good
natured men, third time unlucky to a drunkard (1834)

The Spirits of the Land
for Maggi

The spirits of the land call out to me
They hover in the air, alerting us,
Speaking of old stories yet untold, befitting all

They come in many shapes, tall and round
They cannot be confined to stone or tree
They dance as faeries dance, fiery and free

They live in hope for our redemption
That we will drink them in, embody them
That through our walk they walk the world again

When the Irish and the Scots and Scandinavians came
And the English, God forgives them too,
They carried with them in their hearts their stranger spirits

Most could not see the Old New World spirits sitting in the tree
They planted their own and decorated them with angel dust
Sleeping insecure beneath their many coloured quilts

What is past is present, what is present gives away
The half or darkling sightings of trolls and gnomes
Faeries and elves and all manner of mischievous minx

Perhaps there was a-marrying betwixt the two
The salmon ate the pixie and the brownie ate the bear
Mayhap they sit at table and mutter of the mutants

There is a screech owl in my head and an angel by my bed
A sandman crawls the ceilings and the coyote makes his call
A robin there is a thrush here, the eagle sports a flag

What a wild world, alive with cautionary tales!

To the Moonpie Goddess[1]
or From A to Z

Around about
Bell Buckle
Café
Down below the Mason-Dixon

Events
Force
Grasp

Hungry
Innocents inspire Initiates
Jump into
Karmic fields (of Moonpies) daffodils and day

Lilies, yellow, gold and orange
Miracles (Moonpies)
Nirvana notwithstanding
Operate over time

Proliferate
Questions concerning (Moonpies)
Rehabilitation, refuge, rights, rites
Sanctifying (Moonpies)

Terrestial (Moonpies)
Underlings
Victorious (Moonpies)
Winners

X-rated
Yoginis become
Zodiac
Acrobats
Begin Again in the

Amazing atmosphere of
Bell Buckle
Center

Delight
Enchantment
Fantasy
Gossamer (Moonpies)

History, Hallelujah
Invitation to
J Gregry & Jeannette's Jamboree, include
Kith and kin, no Kickapoo Joy Juice but

Lackadaisical Lady-Bountiful (Moonpie)
Mistress of the (Moonpie) Mysteries[2]
Narnia
On tap

Providing plenty, poets and potters,
Queens of Hearts and Cups
Ruminating runners
Sweetheart songwriters

Timeless (Moonpies)
Undertaker (Moonpies)
Valedictorian (Moonpies)
Wall Street Washington West Point

Xes
Yokels became
Zeroing in on
ABC's, acts born of celestial divinity

[1] ()Brackets indicate where Marauding Magical Moonpies wilfully inserted
themselves into the Broadcast WLIJ AM 1580 reading for the Moonpie
Festival June 19, 1995, ensuring that this poem won First Prize
[2] This one's for Anne White-Scruggs

VE* Day, May 8, 1995 (The Fiftieth Anniversary)
In Memory of My Father Who Died This Day, May 8, 1966

It was a strong day of memories—
Watching the President who fought his own war against war
Watching the Londoners celebrate the end of blitz and despair
The two queens and the princess at Buckingham Palace
No men at their sides. That *was* striking.
The Queen Mother on the verge of tears.
Vera Lynn singing the old song of hope and glory.
No men at their sides, so many had gone to war, so many died.
King George long gone, a young bewildered prince become king
Prince Philip the Consort absent, elsewhere, but ever righteous.
(Princess Margaret's man a man passed over)
These were the three warrior wonen defending Albion
Boudicca, her daughters reborn, honour intact, the Romans vanquished

And those who lived to die for them and their children
Dead or limping proudly in parades, numb to the cost,
Watching from cold bedsits, hospitals and old folks' homes.
Diana wasn't invited, now an unlikely Queen.
The fairy tale was just another cover-up by
Another bewildered prince but who may not be king.
Many miss the passing of an era of ritual fidelity.

When I was a child Elizabeth the princess passed through Toronto.
We watched from high above down upon a clear and serious girl.
The day Winston Churchill died I wrote a eulogy.
My father cried in his cups. He would have been a prince
Disguised as a sailor, a salesman, a social worker,
His unspoken dreams utterly unfulfilled,
He could not wait to celebrate this fiftieth anniversary of VE Day.
Twenty-nine years ago this day he died
In remembrance of what he had lived for:
A Man's Honour, Family, Clan, Country, his King and Queen.

I cannot not speak badly of the dead today.
We stand on their bodies as our children stand on ours
I cannot visit his grave today but we visit together none the less.
I give thanks to one of our glorious Canadian dead,
Along with Americans, British, Russians, so many others.
It was a War we needed to believe in
A Victory we could celebrate.

* For the Very Young, Victory in Europe Day, World War II Commemoration

Alex & Florence Graham (my parents)
– wartime, Halifax, Nova Scotia, Canada

The Land

for Frieda M.

Living here develops a new horizon of insights.
I fold the worn-out English ones away in my closet of conceits.
How shall I imbibe this potent draught of southern moonshine?

It is not the wine. They care less for that.
Nor the whiskey. But the beer contends
It is the ghosts of old dead cowboys in the sultry night

The Land The Land

They came, they took, The Land.
At night they slept round sodden campfires, dreaming The Land.
In the cities they manipulated The Land.

But, you see, they had been driven from The Land.
By Old Troubles, Scots' second sons, Irish daughters, needing The Land.
The last word in every conversation was, the Land.

This they did for their descendants for death overtook them.
This drive was beyond their ability to control, gene-encoded.
Their folly was their greed, forgiveness is their due

For we did it for The Land.

Anasazi doorway in Pueblo Bonito, Chaco Canyon, New Mexico.

PART III:
FRONTIERS

Bells of Revelation

In this country so becoming
This continent beset with broken promises
This planet of token paradoxes

This little solar system is bent on being
Buckled in for a long day's journey into a bright night of stars
Awaiting the bells of revelation

Down deep in the heart of America
Below the Mason Dixon
Alongside the sleeping daffodils

Daffodils outside our house, Spring 1995

The Great Serpent Mound, Chillicothe, Ohio

Brother Woodpecker

Your scarlet skullcap alerts me to the newfound guide
Your precision pecking awakes me to the sacred doorway

Position perfect in line with vision
Lightning tree ruse to my muse

Red feathers mark the good red road
Black dots address the dance design

Called from out my Celtic dream
Delivered to my door, your spirit flies before me

*If only I could tell my people truly
In words that gleamed as bright as southern sunlight
The nature of the task, the beauty of its passage*

*If only I could be as clear as the sound
Of the movement of the stars in the heavens
My voice might speak your message*

*Oh, Brother Woodpecker
I pray you watch over me
Let me not stray from the royal route*

Woodpecker Wise

I did admire the woodpecker
Walking the path beside me.
His colours red and green.
I did broadcast his beauty
His attendance awed me.

The envious Siamese dropped him by my bedroom door.

I did catch passage cross the seas
Pondering his message:
Stop and go.
Fare Well.
Have what you want.
I did depart the Mystic Isle, Merlin's Enclosure
Where wren and woodpecker spell wisdom still.

I do enjoy the newfound southern land
Skies awash with ancestral blood and tears.
Did I forget, though brief, the nature of the task
When the wanting madness spun a tale or two?

Gabbling of my trophies and the journey inward
Circles opened despite my foolish tongue;
Happening upon one of the Old Blood
Her name remembered me and made me sound.

He climbs the tree beside me
His colours red and black.
An ally there to guide me
Calico cat will not attack.

Dream Catchers Are Not What They Seem
for Laura, my niece, & Rance, her husband

Great Spirit looked with pity on Her children down below
Who left their hearts behind them in their hurry to begone
She gathered up her worktools, and made on their behalf
An Image in Her Likeness by which they would well believe

That human life had meaning beyond the daily hunting
She spun a web most wondrous with her super cosmic cunning
This was a very perfect net to catch a perfect runt
Great Spirit danced when She did see the nature of her stunt

But humans were still young and must perforce fall deep asleep.
Dark dreams fell through the web whatever waking they'd aspire
Their Mother's Wheel a magic net to assist their high desire
In the day they wove it willingly Her harvest to acquire

Grand Mother Spider glanced with grace down on Her humankind
And from Her corner of heaven's barn they heard Her speak aloud
"I'll catch the nasty spirits who enter in though not allowed.
My magic circle'll net them one by one or in a crowd."

*Time passed… but then The Mother's Medicine Wheel stopped turning
Trees die, we cry, but the piles of timber keep burning
Seas die, we cry, but the fish are clearly not returning
We die, we cry, we are incredibly undiscerning.*

Despite the death She minds our cries and returns for us to see.
High in some steepled church She mends the web for you and me.
The priest has gone, the people too; this is no victory.
The earth is vast, but we, in debt more than we ought to be.

She gave the wheel, the web, the net, all for our better use.
We wrecked the wheel—rent the web—tore the net—we win the curse
Yet She has been most generous with Her voluminous purse,
And understands that human learning necessitates abuse

She might release us—maybe not—we remind Her of a son.
She casts Her net, repaired, to neatly catch us one by one
She turns the Wheel, it creaks—She oils it till it spins
Cows come home, skylarks soar, eagles nest, all of nature wins.

She turns happy in the heavens, each orb Her bright delight
The Wheel moves, I turn, my kitchen clock shatters on the floor
The postman raps a message on my locked-up front screendoor.
My crafty niece has mailed me a dreamcatcher, maybe more.

One for me, one for he, one for Pandora pussycat, no doubt
Hand-made, imperfect round, beribboned, like earth roundabout
Far far to the north she sits beside her Ojibwa brave
Happy as the day is round, choosing The Mother's nets to save

There is hope because She wove us, She takes us right to heart
Dreamcatcher She re-sent us, to redevelop art
Of weaving, mending and making, and catching good for all
If only we can mind Her just in time to catch Her call.

From the Cherokee Homelands
for the Cherokee amongst us

Cardinal Sun-Worshipper
Bluejay Mischief-Maker
Possum Night-Streaker
Three-Legged Dog-Guarder
Pandora Light-Catcher
Cloaked Messengers in the Heart of America

Taking us to task
Calling us forth
From our green dreams
In the Honey'd Isle
Awakening us to new songs
Otherworlds in the Cherokee Homelands

New friends dancing in the dark
Bright fires in old eyes
Bright Wing Eagle Your Talking Stick
Drums the circle of our heart
Dream-catchers are not what they seem
In the Waiting-Room of the Medicine Teachers

LeRoy's Cabinets

for Ange & Ron

Down a backroad, longside a field, close by a friend,
Lies a landmark at the crossroads
Each time I pass I want to enter in, discover who and why,
But would my mystery fly away or even deeper lie?

Who is LeRoy and what sort of cabinets can he make?

I hear the song I am the bait I am the fish
The myths of Middle Tennessee rise up around me,
Cicadas tell long tales, crickets wind them up,
And I am running free in a field of golden grasses

Is LeRoy the maker of the myths, the carpenter of form?

*Was he here before us all
Watching Creek and Cherokee battle for their holy hunting grounds?
Is he the Master Builder, or Joseph with his blooming staff,
Maker of magical boxes within boxes, our final drawers?*

One day the King of Kings will have come upon my form,
Made a cabinet befitting me, a trunk full of treasure and delight
I will meet his eye, and say, I always meant to come on in,
You took the measure of my needs, the dimensions of my deeds

We've changed LeRoy's name, but the building is there...

Hunting Grounds
Regarding Bedford and Rutherford Counties, Tennessee

These were their holy hunting grounds
Here, where we have made camps of wood and brick and glass
Parked our 6 & 8 cylinder unhorse-powered cars and trucks
Where we bay at the illusory light of the moon of commerce
Day and night, year after year, divining markets, counting shells

We are not so different.
We bleed and laugh and breed, we love and die
We make mistakes and pay, empires rise and fall
But we settle where they dared not, and I wonder why?
Even Corn grows better beyond this Sacred Circle

This land has a mind of its own, a destiny that drew us,
Like them, but we can grow where once seabeds were,
We manage space in time by the marvelous Works of Man,
Invent, manipulate and pioneer beyond belief
A Master Race, casting tall shadows in the suspicious dust

Tall trees grow where once great creatures swam
Four-leggeds prance imprisoned on manicured rectangles
Two-leggeds lie in service to the ethic of an outworn cult
The eagles and other vultures keep an eon watch upon us all
And green, green grow our moneytrees, sad envy of the world

We are diligent, long-suffering, outcasts from the Old.
Our pallor stretches far back to short northern summertime,
To far eastern steppes, where we rode, bravehearts everyone.
We brought our urge to freedom packed inside Pandora's box
Along with greed and a host of other gene encoded clocks

We, like they, were hunters: a different time, a different place,
Driven west, across the Sea, by the confines of islands, continents,
We followed the fateful Roman road of power, lines in time.
We hunted the hunters and now we hunt our selves.
The world turns round to face us as we eat the world alive

Yet, growing deep within us, here on their holy hunting grounds
An urge to craft a magic circle of protection and delight
As once their sleek fox-eyed shaman did, to nurture the good
And restrain the evil, to balance the budget of planetary spending
So green and golden is the hope we harvest here
On these holy hunting grounds

In A Woman's Body
for the Chers amongst us

I inhabit a woman's body.
It has been immense fun accessing it,
Playing and working in it
Fiddling with the works, the parameters

If I had chosen a man's, if I could have,
It might have been much different, maybe so
Career and business could have claimed my brain
Even the stock market might have mattered some

I was born a woman before these startrek times,
In the 40's, when women knew their place
Doing men's work whilst men died to play at war
With warrior wrens and wacs and waves and many more

I would not be a nurse, I would not be a nun
I would not play charades, I would not play at chess
Ivory towers looked grey, skyscrapers weren't high enough
I read as much as possible, I taught to see the light

I left my cage and travelled round the world,
I planted trees and cooked for friends
I made circles in the dust, held children when they cried
I was a woman being becoming more so everyday

I inhabit my woman's body, 52 and climbing,
I stretch it out and bounce it, I am determined to be fit
I cuddle up to husband and ask him sweetly for a little bit
I think I'm doing grandly. I sure as hell won't quit.

Madame Tennessee: Between Spring and Summer
for David & Jane

Driving down Highway 82 her daffodils are dying
Blossoms white and pink giving way to red and yellow
A lush green carpet being laid across her countryside
Her People coming out to play

And I a Newcomer caught between spring and summer
In love with the mystery of Madame Tennessee

It's hot but I am told she's hardly warming up
Her heat enfolding me, priming me for later days
My calves and thighs and wings are cooking well
A young spring chicken turning on her spit

Me, an Incomer bestriding spring and summer
Being loved by the magic of Madame Tennessee

Who can tell where all her music and joy will take me
In a land where ecstasy comes easily to mind
And happiness is measured by the absolute extension of your Drawl
Where truth and beauty have good ground in which to grow

Mound Minders
In Recognition of The Guardians

One has to be called.
One has to hear.
One has to follow.

In which case, be careful
Where you tread and why
How you speak and when.

If one is fortunate, one learns to listen.
The guardians of The Mound may speak.
They may send Messages to decode.

In which case, be awe full
About your business, your play
Take no chances not worth taking

If one is blesséd, one succeeds
The guides befriend and follow us home
They spin circles of goodness roundabout

In which case you are committed
To weaving beautiful webs for them to adorn
To speaking the truth for lies won't do

If one is moved from place to place
Shown sacred sites and told to be ware
How matter and spirit work as one

You are the bearer of mysteries
You are more than you mind
You are a meeting place

Passage to Pinson

[Spring equinox]
The day was hot and dry, daffodils blooming.
Trees bare but bushes glowing. Skyblue and daring.
Wild garlic and sleeping kudzu.

[Passage]
Flea markets infected with junk
A dismal welcome from a wayside Lone Wolf.
A land desecrated by oil companies and bad breath.

[Arrival]
Every hill a mound in disguise
The museum too. Always suffering the lost raiders.
A fat boy taking his medicine badly, a nightmare initiation.

[Discovery]
Saul's Mound. Men Only. No feet touch the ground.
Thirty mounds. Three call. Pray. Hearsay.
Where once temples lay, trees grow, lovers play.

[Message]
From the stillness, spirit breeze blows.
From their timeless world the guardians appear to grant
The age-old gift of tobacco to give again.

[Realization]
It is so powerful, this real work of the Spirit.
The dimensions crack, open the church doors.
The light floods the nave. That cross was a tree.

[Fare Well]
Do not walk that return lest the other snake awake.
Go forward, await. Christie brings me a glass of ice water.
Her father, an old soldier, rocks on his swing, telling history.

[Future]
We have guardians wherever we go, marking time
We shall not want for inspiration or livelihood
Only do The One Work and All Shall Be Well

Swan Songs of the Celtic Soul
for Marty

Thick and sweet, rivers of love and loss.
Pour through hill and dale, city street and country road
Carrying us cross the seas to the Old World

Advancing in couples, squares and lines
Short skirts, chevron shirts and cowboy boots
Bringing alive a past that never was

The moccasins are buried
The old chiefs asleep and dreaming
The greatgrandchildren awake in the nightmare

Media saloons sport the vision traumatic
Remaking history, gilding the common coin.
The truth was colder, meaner, harder.

The survivors
Rekindle manifest destiny
Rewind the West

Songs of the gods and their heroes
They came on horseback across the Steppes
In covered wagons across the European Mainland
With the pioneers across the Great Plains

Swan songs of the Celtic Soul, the Saxon Spirit
Viking Bravery

Tales from the Navajo
for Sam Small Eagle

He saw me coming
I was moderately prepared
To be his ally

His face was weathered, cracked open
Like the canyon walls, their colour in sunlight
Red brown gold

His eyes indefinable.
He said his wife was all white
And I was welcome into his many mansions.

I recalled that dimension,
Different, rounder than paleface time,
Multi-faceted, turning to meet itself.

We sat on the mesa top on the rockface
Discussing wars and bloodlines and possibilities
His kin hovered around us, waiting for money to pass palms

The journey unfolded, like the slabs of rock, rough
And smooth, no step the same, everything unexpected
The damp sand collected around my bare toes. I was home.

The two men bonded over the eagle's eye
The dark became light, the sun set, the Star Nation waking
The odour of pine and cooling rock, pungent and healing

There was a price to pay, the Canyon spirit would have it
The souls of those long dead cried out still
We prayed, standing; Christ, he said, would sacrifice the world

He was not a Christian. He was Navajo.
His life, his ancestors, his heritage, his Spirit.
Che! The Canyon echoed back its own name, meeting itself.

Three eagles, we flew along the steep plateau
Guests of the ancestors and the Star Nation.
Forgiveness in time, but the Canyon would have us descend

Deeper into the mysteries. Spirits of sacred places
Know our needs. Alone, I would have descended in the bright
darkness.
But for the moment, we must rise back to this upper world

To meet familiar selves, to hold together the semblance of self.
We must give up fear in such places and trust our guide
Who had moved through time and was his own ancestor enemy:

Anasazi, the Old People the New People replaced
And then came Kit Carson and the killing of the innocents.
The Canyon rejected them. Our paler feet were the first

On that place since those boots of betrayal
If our hearts had not been pure, the Spirit of Che
Would have tossed us over the edge, as the brave Navajo woman

Took her assailant to his death, there below where
They ploughed their fields and birthed babies
Like Sam himself, seventy-odd years since

A wiry warrior, a tall man of peace and a woman who would be
Warror and peacemaker, we journeyed into the Canyon de Che
To make peace with one another, to manifest destiny.

Never underestimate the magic of the sacred place of power
To transform the drunk and disorderly, the cowardly,
The starstruck, into real people or small flying eagles

*After returning from a Magical Journey into the Navajo Nation, to Canyon de
Chelly, Arizona, May 30, 1995*

The Hogan
for the Navajo medicine men (May 30, 1995)

Dark and round, bright and limitless,
Earth and tree.We have come home to the Ancestors.
We bear food to the medicine men and the patient people.

The objects of power: eagle feathers, rattle,
Subjects speaking through the dim light into my old mind
Remembering me to my great great grandmother

Her name hides awaiting, buried by a wounded people
Bent by multiple betrayals, white mischief passing through them
Did she pass for white, as the ways of the palefaces

Passed like dark clouds into their minds.
Their penultimate revenge: Breed into, defeat from within
The enemy who kills by booze, smallpox, guns and religion.

It is almost unbearable. But it must be borne.
The robe of remembrance is cast over me.
I am all peoples. Grandfather Bear welcomes me home.

The old people lie in the circle of light, crooked and weary
From battling life on the reservation, Out of America.
Here in the Navajo Nation, in a circle of power, they heal

One another, wary faces demanding justice as did their forebears
I dissipate out into the round earthen walls
The parts of my selves willing chalices of pain.

The young medicine men listen gently to the old man
Who tells tales of the Spirit of the Canyon
How it is possible for even such as we to understand.

This timeless bridgemaker between worlds
Fighting paleface battles, putting in time as a Patriot
Before returning home with his white Pennsylvanian wife

Gifting his seven children into the starstriped melting pot
Getting back to the business of being his grandfather's son
Farming the canyon floor and the mesa top, meeting alien visitors

Hoping for one or two who would hear his song. We did.
In the hogan the fires of the Navajo Nation are burning alive
The eagle feathers reach out for waiting hearts.

Old Man, Queen of Heaven
for Peter Caddy, 1917–1994

The sun deepens in the southern way,
Layers of orange and peach and apple red.
Eden re-opens her gates, offers her trees,
Recalling us home to original delights

My child runs green and naked in the grey Atlantic rain
North is south, time stands still, the spindle turns,
My father's face is round and good, sword in hand
My mother's dark and deep, the war has passed

Life is a roundabout and we're inside out
Learning lessons till we die of knowledge.
Brother hears my plea and Persephone arises from a watery grave
Sister, bitter in her wound, marks me for a whore

I am dark and sweet.
Fallen from the tree of life.
Where Lilith sits in grace
Bequeathing Sister Eve her lot

I shall play until she drops me
I shall dare all when she awakes
The sun is her golden chariot,
The man in the moon her son

She sets to give us thought.
She turns to care for others.
Too much light can destroy.
Too much darkness deathen.

In the garden Apollo and I dance together.
The Olympians gaze amazed.
We shall stride alien worlds.
We shall birth a new civilisation

The old man in the new garden[1]
speaks of the stations of the cross

The nature spirits rise at dawn to greet us.
The elementals make peace to give us grace.
The Angel of Findhorn is born.
The Vision of Albion embodied.

Remember to re-member, the old man[2] *said*
who travelled many worlds on his magic carpets

The old man who was not
On the Roman bus where all roads lead
Who had his say in many tongues

I did not forget

The sun shines and sets
Deep down into these southern lands
Where shamans once spoke with rattlesnakes
And the Queen of Heaven had Her rightful place

*The old man[3] marked out the lineaments of the Star Nation
On the Anasazi ground his ancestors died on for*

Trees remember more
Spiral-speak of pyramidal shapes
Plateaus against the horizon
Mounds in memory of the principal peoples

*An old man waits for me inside the Mound of his choice
He sends his messengers to guide me well*

[1] Peter Caddy, Co-Founder of the spiritual community in North East Scotland, the Findhorn Community
[2] Gurdjieff, author, spiritual teacher and carpet merchant
[3] Sam Small Eagle, veteran and spiritual teacher

Peter Caddy shown with the author, outside her house in Somerset

Tornado Watch[1]

To the nature spirits in memory of Findhorn and Roc[2]

Around the kitchen table we discuss
What to do, where to go, when the animals signal
That an aberrant act of nature is on its way.
Never why, for what is the point?

All the hard work of a lifetime
Lost in mere seconds, security, sense of order.
Perhaps the cast iron bathtub remains
Remindful that purification might be on purpose

Who knows? They can track them
And tell us on the Weather Channel
But only your cat or dog knows the true direction
Of a tornado's intent, their wilderness intact.

No wonder the South still holds onto God
God only knows who will come next to His Court
Spinning tales of earthly woe and deliverance
The wilful and the weak alike at His Mercy

The Wizard of Oz lies at the end of a twister's tail
Waiting to impart mysteries to ponytailed girls
He has lured into his funnel to the sky
But even he appears not to be aware of why

Of course, science knows why but not whyfor
Knows the makeup, the costume
But not the exact play of the monster missive,
Another spiral message from the old gods

Perhaps they watch from above down through
Their tunnel telescope into our kitchen sinks
Amazed at the waste and corruption we slough
Off in the name of advancing civilization

And in fine celestial anger without recourse
To the New God who lead us this way into the desert
They turn round the dial to ten or so
And their cosmic backs on the consequences

Like in the old movies of Zeus and Jason
Juno and Medea and the warrior skeletons
Come to life to fight battles out of time
Humans are a helpless lot against such Games

When their spaceships land in our backyards
We cannot speak with eachother out of ancient awe
We have this certain feeling they walk amongst us still
Assessing our secret wishes to serve, our selfishness

We can only watch tornadoes safely in our dreams
Or on video, hoping we won't be online next
Or maybe we can cater to unseen elementals
Catching their drift as they play next us in the moonlight

And like our ancestors before the Fall
Place dishes of fresh white milk out for the faeries
Dress our boys in pretty blouses to confuse the pixies
And prick up our ears when elves are mentioned

Whatever we do, life is a risky turn of affairs
In the lands where tornadoes hover and spin
Seeking out human sacrifices

[1] Written days after experiencing an excruciating dream about tornadoes and
several conversations with Southern friends accustomed to living with them.
[2] The Findhorn Community (my home for several years) in Northeast
Scotland was founded and is still dedicated to cooperating with the inner or
hidden as well as the outer forces of Nature. Roc is the name of the scientist-
mystic who had deep experiences with the nature spirits and inspired the
Founders and all later residents and visitors.

Shamans of Myselves
for my brothers: Bob, Ralph & Ian

Sculpted mound meets sky above me
Flattened top holds known mysteries
Evened steps take my measure
Opened doors receive my spirit

Snake skins abandoned before me
Old selves begging our forgiveness
Keepers of the mound rattle us
Pierced with clarity, caring less

One touches my head. I am dead
Old skins waken flesh forgotten
Old memories flood minds out of time
Feet find solid ground place out of space

Battles we won and lost pass through
We wear each skin to size and shape
Lion, deer, coyote, fox, bear
Our fur reflects relentless sun

The air holds us firm as we fly
Feathers akin to rainbowarcs
Cardinal, chickadee, cuckoo, crow, eagle
We hunt, we sing, we disappear

We swim in long silver waters
Sun and moon opalescent orbs
Trout, shark, catfish, perch and salmon
We stream, schools adrift with seamen

We walk under the mutant clouds
Wish for worlds we will inherit
Astride all lands under one sun
Painting stories on rock, fur, tree

When we are done the holy round
We wheel up into formation
One soul, spirit, many bodies
Redeemed in the light of passage

Unsteady, down uneven steps
Weathered from winters of neglect
I turn, tobacco found, given,
Shamans of myselves at peace again

Arising from a restored Kiva at Kelly Place near Mesa Verde, Colorado.